To, Too M

A Collection of Moments

Weatherspoon

For my mothers, all of them.

"Because my heart is in the future and I know where I belong,
It just takes time."
- Jon Bellion

"In the valley of the blind, the one-eyed man is king."
- August Wilson

Contents

Preface: The Moral Authority of Monsters

It all started in the metro hospital in a poor city. A baby boy came weeping out of his mother into distilled air. A large baby he was, 8 pounds 12 ounces. His mother pressed him up against her chest, a connection made visible, finally after nine months. She named him King, said he was special, and prayed over him. At least that's how I imagine I happened. I wouldn't have any way of knowing, or rather, I can never bring myself to remember what I was there to see. Perhaps the loss of memory or gaps in consciousness exists within us primarily to stress the unimportance of the past. But unfortunately, the past is most of what I've written about here. History has its place, beyond value, in the eye of the beholder.

Behold the unimportance of an inner-city kid who has always wanted more than he could ever help himself to. Give him a chance; I think you might like him.

I hope my arrogance is more familiar than offensive. Consider this text a mirror pretending to be a window as I, a young Black boy, writes in pitiful wonder of himself and of the miracles he might be able to perform if excellence weren't such an extreme sport for his kind, in America. Consider this a message to too many children who must feel the same as I feel and have felt, or worse, feel nothing at all. Maybe it's the teenage blood in my veins, the 17 years of structure crumbling as I reach for pieces of manhood, but every time I come across an apologist, a racist, a denier of a painfully clear past, a fraction of my understanding for my fellow man, woman, and peer diminishes. I devolve into a sickness, a detachment, a moral apathy that is most attributed to the White men and women of old. It's a monsterdom that preys on the victimhood of the conscience. For ages, it has controlled the heart of

America and has rotted the minds and principles of great leaders. It manifests itself as willful ignorance of humanitarian struggles--a list of political priorities and gestures rather than human equality and wholeness throughout. This sickness is liable to overtake anyone who has been hurt before and gives faux moral authority to the empowered victims we come to know as monsters.

> My psychologist asked me once
> If I've ever been bullied,
> And I explain
> In a flash of thoughts,
> One two, one two,
> Swing left and right,
> Don't die,
> Just breathe.

My older brother taught me to fight when I was 8 and there I was at 10 practicing broken ribs and jawbones. Peer pressure was more real than ever then. The day I decided to root for the other team because the other team was larger. How scary the snowy earth can be when tinted red and validation had run away with Summer. Winter was there early, and I remember this failure, vividly. I guess I should say a little something about bullying first, and how I agree that it exists, but you see in Black neighborhoods, you're not a victim until you're a casualty, until you earn your spot on the local news featuring a dark bag, a statistic, and anyone who might have loved you. As a result, fights are commonplace, but no one dares to call themselves a victim, so the problems are never really solved, and those communities become engrossed in anger, a war zone of sorts. My cousin and I were smack-dab in the middle of one of those communities, one of those wars. We were trapped in a pair of smiles, and other moments where our bodies weren't our own. Our interests suddenly became that of everyone else's. Elementary school teachers prophesied that we could only ever be products of our environments, products of war, and something about an old White man named Maslow and what we needed. It's a bang out, y' know? At the end of every school year, on the last day, all the cliques get together and take out their problems on one another. Like a middle school edition of the purge, only, last years' was canceled by the bats so we marked up this winter edition to make up for lost time. What a scene it was, Black skin against bone, and teeth flying free against the fierce winter breeze, the peace of chaos, and blood that felt like home filled us. And still, I can't remember what a bully looks like, underneath the predator in every cry for help. In response to my psychologist, I said,

"I don't think I've ever been bullied, but if I have it's complicated."

My psychologist said back to me,

"Well, what about your mom? How is that relationship?"

I said,

"Which one," and devolved into an intrinsic conflict about filiality.

Children are like legal ornaments during the week of Christmas, no one cares if a few are broken by the end of it, as long as the tree is put up and made to look pretty. And when said ornamental children dare forsake the tree from which they fall, they are shunned, and cursed, and dealt with, until they are forgotten by the presumed and already accepted moral authority of its rigid structure. The experiences made me think of what I wouldn't give to be a good son, both to my mothers and my country. The list happens to be literal,

> My sense of self and self-worth,
> Individuality,
> Unearned respect,
> My voice and passion,
> My white friends,
> The victory I feel when I get to sleep
> Without crying.
> My peace.

My aunt is Filipino, married into my biological family. She's a wife to my uncle and mother to my cousin. The second time I was taken away from my biological mother by DCFS, I landed in her care. I was nine years old, and I'll never forget how while I was there, she treated me like a child--an idea so foreign to my past self. She was never authoritative with me, only highly suggestive, which inspired a peculiarly begotten respect, a kind I had never seen myself give before. She told me I couldn't watch the cartoons I liked, and that I couldn't play the 3rd person shooting games I'd sworn by in those days; said I was too young to be watching and playing those things. I suppose looking back at it, I was sort of offended. By the time I was placed in her care, I had already survived two shoot-outs and had watched a grown man die a bloody death on a sidewalk. I wasn't sure that SpongeBob and Call of Duty were the largest influences in my life then, but my aunt did and she did away with them. I didn't argue.

She made a mean chicken adobo, and I found myself obsessed with her cheddar biscuits. My cousin and I would play chess at the dining room table after we did our homework and occasionally listened to Owl City on his laptop; he taught me the game, and how to like pop music. He also lent me his Harry Potter and Diary of A Wimpy Kid collections. I went to a nice public school as well. These were odd times for me, taste breakers of sorts, world-changing inconstants that would foreshadow my life as it is now: White & Black and full.

My uncle though, he grew tired of me. I could always tell he didn't want me. I'm not sure what my biological mother paid him to take me and keep me, but one day, however much it was, it wasn't enough. He got as angry with me as I had ever seen him. As I was getting ready for school I'd accidentally flooded the toilet, which flooded the bathroom floor, and eventually seeped down into the basement. It was not a fun time overall. After that, he yelled

"Pack your shit!" Like thunder, like something that wanted to hurt me, and called my biological mother. Just like that my life had changed once more.

The good news was that I could play as much Call of Duty and watch as much Spongebob as any prepubescent boy might want to, the bad news was that life was all bad again. I wonder now if my uncle knew he was sending me to die, if my aunt had any say, what my cousin thought. I don't fault them, any of them, they gave me some of the best moments of my life, some of the best food, and a taste of something slightly better than chicken adobo and cheddar biscuits: *Family*. I wouldn't find access to that feeling for another five years after that, but then I lost that too.

I said to my psychologist,

"That kind of instability gave me the greatest potential for evil. Just people giving up on me, it hurt. I wanted everyone else to feel just how bad it hurt, so we could have that one thing in common and I wouldn't feel so alone."

In the years following, after I was kidnapped by my biological mother and before I was taken from her once more, she had a boyfriend named Moses. One who taught me business amongst other things. The closest thing I had to a father was my mother's partner, irony strikes the stepfather who never stepped away from kids he didn't make. He gave me the birds and the bees talk, but really the lot of us were lions and tigers, I mean the stakes were higher and maturity comes after experience, not necessarily with it because admittedly I set the bar for stupid those days.

I miss those days.

We'd play NBA 2K, eat popsicles, and run around our neighborhoods like we didn't have good sense; we didn't to be honest--no one taught us that. But there's a beauty in that which went up in smoke when we began to trade pieces of ourselves for escape. The girls we loved growing up became hoes because we stopped--loving them, I mean. Our boys began to wear their pants like ankle weights, like shackles, like they were tired of running, but they'd pull them up to escape a siren. We were all so concerned with feeling, with euphoria, with smoke, with each other. I wish I could give you a single memory, a single fault in urban communities, in my education, but all of it is relative and interwoven.

Why is everything you write so sad?

I was thirteen years old when the inquiry first landed. My answer was then as it is now. To an unfamiliar audience, it's a sad story, but to me, I'm reflecting, remembering, coping, and understanding the mechanics of disillusionment and reality and why they always lead us to different ends. Why the unfamiliar are cursed with curiosity and why I have so many answers for them.

My psychologist said, "Wow, that must have been hard." She validated my feelings but pushed me to move on. So I moved on, physically. I planted myself in a garden of sorts, where everything grows, everything is beautiful and just getting started, so that nothing is ready to die. It's a private high school, a white place in color and context. I'm a scholarship kid now, but not entirely--I mean that is what I am but only a piece, I'm half monster, half amazing these days, but also Black, fat, and underage, so naturally, with time and education I've developed morals but haven't quite come into my authority yet--my adoptive mother paid what my scholarship didn't until the end of my junior year, until now. She said to me,

I'm going to treat you like the man you want to be so badly.

She ended up treating me so badly.

Henceforth are a collection of moments,
From the depths and the pain
And the best of my memory.

Henceforth is a mix of what I know
And how I hurt.
The poetry of my flesh,
Like an arm, but of greater function,
Of greater need.

Henceforth are my lungs,
It's my liver,
It's my heart,
And on them are secrets
I learned by living.

To, Too Many Children

Europa: A Wide Face

Let Me

Let me learn you a lesson in the hopes that it protects you,
And maybe gets you to heaven.
Let me fall on this sword in front of you,
So you don't have to pay out of pocket for points of view
Too many children do.

Remember,
Young is a circumstance,
Not a personality.

We Say He Passed Away

We say he passed away,
Which I hate,
Because it sounds less like he's dead
And more like he missed his bus stop
Or something--

I wonder if the driver
Would be so kind
As to wait on an empty corner
And take my cousin's ghost
To the rec center to play basketball
One last time.

The Disconnect

The disconnect is no Dad in the home,
Feeling alone is only natural,
After the facts have come in,
About what really happened when you were younger.

You're no one's dummy or druggy,
You're just lost in experience and book smarts,
It's like, the more you know,
The easier you fall apart,

And what's worse is, you'll get older,
Before you ever even start
To cope with being young
But also being as smart as you are.

Call Me Dumb If You Want

So call me dumb if you want.
Call me young,
And lump me in with the bunch of
Fun loving,
Drug taking bums,
You see so much these days.

Tell me how much you hate me
For embracing my culture
To change it.

Somebody has to do right by us,
And that somebody isn't,
Your generation.

Between Us

Love is not so short a feeling
That it fits between us.
We are in it,
The way we are in the world.

Stuck In The Middle

Like is too juvenile a word,
Love is too old.
So we're stuck in the middle
As children often are,
With everywhere to go but home.

Dear Mama

Dear Mama, I know that,
You need love and gas money.
You need time and a little something on the light bill.
You need a hug and some groceries.
And you know that emotional and material balance
Is not impossible,
But it feels so damn close to it.

I've never been blind to your struggles,
And I know I don't feel the weight
Of things like you do,
But my heart breaks the same.

Silence

A simple structured story,
A budding boastful byline
A longing to communicate
That necessitates the opening
Of an Oxford dictionary
Believe me when I say that
Growing up I was never a smart boy
I had to learn, like you, but much later
And much faster.
I read until I knew how to write,
I wrote until I knew how to speak,
I spoke until I realized how powerful
My silence could be.

My People Can't Afford To Pay Attention

February like,
My people can't afford to pay attention
No more,
With white teachers in black schools,
We're in detention,
We're bored.

February like,
"I'm sorry officer,"
Martin had a dream,
And he must have been sleepwalking 'cuz,
Tonight is like tomorrow night on the Eastside,
Except 3 more people died.
I could cry or I could tell you about it.
And ask questions like,
We've come so far, but where are we going?

Ameri, caucasian prince as big as Mutombo,
Hope you don't struggle,
He'll put a bullet in your back
And hide the gun smoke

Freedom, I hope you don't miss it,
We might not see it again,
Great is not the name of this land.

Progress, maybe,

But what's 50 years
In the face of our 400-year legacy?

What's black skin to music?
And commands like "move it"
From white people,
Excuse us if we dance a little while we do it.
This skin of mine is a rhythm,
A riot, and a movement.

Our blood runs a dark red just like yours--
And our blood is precious, just like yours,
And we can't afford to spill any more of it.

3/5ths of a man no more.
No more equal but separate,
No more ego-tripping politicians
Twisting the government to their benefit,

No more masters,
No more Kings,
Confederate flags or leather beams,
No more "Because I said so"
No more "I can't read,"

My love letter to February,
Though, I'm black every month,
And as scary as that is,
I'm happy to be me.

Platinum Blonde Hair

You're imperfect as hell,
And I know you knew we could tell,
You're reckless and rude,
And aggressive, but true and respected,
Because you are who you are,
And that's so hard to do.

I've Met Your Friends

I'll never try to tell you how to live,
Though, pretty ain't what pretty is,
I mean, I've met your friends,
And they talk about your body a lot,
Said it's a nice one,

Sometimes the lowest compliments
Feel like the highest.

It's Because I'm Shy

I feel I'd have to cover my ears to compliment you
Or close my eyes
To love what you look like,
It's not because you're not beautiful,
It's because I'm shy.

You are the only one I could be that for,

Freestyle

Immortality, a sin of nature,
Betrayal, sin of man,

My brother said I couldn't know power,
Until offered yoga & tonic water
By white bitches off Instagram.

I've got a red-hot demon in me,
I got a couple niggas needin' Jesus in me,
Not the man but the idea,
I know you seen it in me.
They wanna hang a bad nigga,
So we keep it friendly.

Let peace be a way and not an order,
Bunch of marches for our freedom,
Now our fuckin' feet sore
And
Give a fuck less bout a tv
Got niggas everywhere screamin'
"Free Me!"
Got us callin' women bitches,
'Cuz it was advertised as "PG"

Black history in a theater,
Don't clap after--
'Cuz it's a riot when you leave

Hurt niggas wanna clap at ya.

Don't dare act like you don't know
That our teachings have been backward.
America taught us violence,
Now we think we'll teach the classes.

Gang-Gang or Baldwin

You can't bring poetry to a fistfight, for sure,
But you can't swing at life either.
Pick your poison and live.
I pray that silence hits you before someone else does,
Before reality.
Around here common sense is like gravity
And if you're not in chains every day
You're breaking the law.

Questions

Have you ever met a dark room
With feelings?
With walls that need help
A little more than you do?

Has anything ever taught you silence,
Like a funeral?
A wedding reception?
A doctor's appointment?

Which comes first in a young man's life
Anyway?

I'm shook,
And I wake up sort of pretentious
These days.
Like I got answers, like I ain't scared,
But I've always been scared.

The Saddest Thing You'll Ever Hear

The saddest thing you'll ever hear is that
Your friend doesn't believe in love,
And that life might be okay without it,
Because you'll wonder who taught them to settle,
And who taught you to move.

Better Love

My brother told me once,
That his girlfriend left him for someone else,

I said to him, sadly,
That we compete with comfort
For better love,
Not with people.

Disorder

To pimp a smile.
Make me laugh and I'm yours, until the world barks,
Or 'til it's my turn to howl at the moon again.
My attention is fleeting, but my passions remain.
I think I got a disorder.

Enoughness

I was writing this science fiction short story in the 6th grade,

When one of my characters said something
I think is incredible as I was writing him.

He said,

"Build yourself a well of love to drink from when you're low,
So that your lows may always be high above
Who you were when you drank after other people."

And I've been different ever since.

In the context of the story,
this particular character practiced a very powerful
And ancient love magic called
Enoughness.

Suffice it to say that I've always been a very weird boy,
With a wild imagination
Suffice it to say that I've always had an inkling for the
transcendental--
I've always been more than the rumble in my stomach
When we didn't have enough to eat,

More than the weed I smoked,
And the liquor I sipped in between
Sharing my insides with my toilet bowl.
More than the thick skin I grew to fend off the bad shit
I passed through on my incredible journey here--

To something taller than an inner-city street light
To something more beautiful than the doves at my little cousin's
funeral,
To this place of divine increase,
At the feet of Dionysus, loose sexuality, androgyny,
White debater kids who look and sound a little too good to be true.

This is what we call enoughness,
A powerful capitalist magic
Also known as middle to upper-class America.
Private institutions,
Money-making,
Dreams to young chasers,
A larger more luxurious fishbowl
Inside the largest well.

It's only once or twice between every now and then
That I remember how no one ever taught me to swim,
How I come from the mud, how I actually need air to breathe,
It's only every now and then that I realize
Just how far I had gotten from home,
How I was only supposed to drink from that well,

And not jump in.

How To Grow Up Without A Father

1) Rehearse your last name until it means something to you.
2) Love your mom, and anyone who feels like her.
3) Cry into your pillow, talk to God, tell him to take your voice and make it deeper.
4) Wonder if you are gay.
5) Watch all of Steve Harvey's videos on YouTube
6) Hit the gym, hit someone, hurt yourself until you feel like something someone could abandon.
7) When someone tells you that it's not your fault, listen
8) Everything is going to feel like your fault. The responsibility will make you arrogant, almost narcissistic, but be kind, and humble, always. Not just when it suits you.
9) Wake up with the kind of hole your chest that your mother can't feed,
   And a hospital can't fix.
10) Find work, find purpose, find art, and appreciate it.
    Appreciate it so much that you become it,
    That you become the things you love most.

That is how you grow up without a father.

Infatuation Is The Plastic of Loves

Less than human, but more than God,
Little magic.
A product of infatuation--
The plastic of loves.
Like lust in place of care
Or wings too small,
To fly to your forever with.

She looks at you like
She wants to try you on.
An exotic creature,
You are something holy,
To a catholic girl.

The fetishization of Black men
In white spaces
Is flattering, until it hurts.

I've Always Needed The Help

Grimey like New York and sweet like Tucson,
Like cheddar Bob and biscuits,
Like dumb mistakes below the waist,
And love for the wrong women.

Maybe I should work on myself,
I've always needed the help,
I'm always there for whoever else
And never here for myself,

I never hear from myself,
Not until I'm burning like the bush
In the oldest book on my shelf,
God, I needed this.

Pray For The Home Staying Friend Of A Gypsy

Pray for the home staying friend of a gypsy,
Even if sour distances
Make sweet memories.

I'm not content to lead that type of life,
I need my solid few
Or nothing's right.
Everything is loose if nothing's tight.

I lose sleep over my group,
Just about every night.

Grown Folks' Business

I'd like to talk about how old I had gotten so young.
How readily the fast-paced times partook of their share of my development,
I think it's true that all I really know is what I feel in my bones,
And the rest I'm just remembering, or possibly even making up.

I struggle to the edge of my bed and wonder if this is the "grown folks' business"
My mother had so vehemently asked me out of--
The head aching existentialism in knowing.
The responsibility. the maintenance, the get-up-and-go, the heartache.
I thought she was being exclusive,
But she was merely being miserable and preferred to do it alone
Or at least in older, harder, harsher company.

Some who knew how to dance, and laugh,
And play cards from the bottom of their tired hearts.
Still, mama can't acknowledge how she fathered us wrong.

Cursed single parentage heritage, homes built on a prayer,
Bellies full of sleep and fists full of fight,
Mama made the hard times mean something,
'Cuz mama made the hard times harder.
If this is, in fact, the grown folks' business,
Do I dare attempt my inheritance so soon?

Split

What I don't want Is a kind of dull life with sharp happenings.
I won't wander into the thick of things as something smaller than
the thought of tomorrow.
In science we learn to split the subjective into objective digestible
bits--
My country asks that I do that with my name.
African-American:
A curriculum taught by life and made out of skin,
The darker brother,
Forbidden knowledge,
A sort of national sin.
If only I were half as dark as my every tomorrow has been
I might understand.

Georgia Peach Tree

Relationships are shaky,
I know and embrace it,
Sorry, I wasted your time,
An extroverted, claustrophobic
Feeling, like love,
It don't come easy.

It grows like a Georgia peach tree
When it's big, it's beautiful,
When it's not
People step on it
I sort of stepped on you,
And I'll learn from it.

Apostles

Don't waste your time on apostles,
Go straight to the source.
People be actin' whole, but they weak at the core,
God, one thing you never spend is time,
Turned water to wine,
Got alcoholics swarming like the demons inside 'em
Had you turned water to apple cider,
You'd have had a better people behind you.

I lost my father to your magic trick,
You lost a brother to the shit you did,
Phony access to a richer mix,
Wonder why Judas needed 30 pieces of silver then?

To re-up.

Heroes

Pray that God protects the land
If its heroes are too peaceful,
For they choose to save their souls
Over their people.

Is it right of us to pray
Instead of exercising evil?

Can't we do both?

If I Needed Someone

The truth is,
As the fates and irony would have it,
If I needed someone
To believe me,
I would have lied.

Envy

All I do is hope, because of that I know heartbreak well.
Disappointment is the birth of envy
Because I start to think the grass is greener everywhere else.
And then I remember,
How young I am to feel that way.

Everything is urgent these days,
Because we're all kids who want things.
Envy: the sin of my city.

A year ago, I met a girl that I can't have.
I met love & reason in the same place,
In the same person,
And I watched as they fought
Until one of them disappeared.

16 years ago, I met a city that I can't help,
And brothers, who wore their masculinity
Like a straight Jacket,
See, they want things too
But they could never free their hands
To reach out and grab it.

I don't remember when,
But I met anxiety too,

Cousin to fear, in love with depression,
Obsession is something we all deal with,
I think.
I know I think too much.
I want to stop, but I want a lot of things.

Things, like hope,
And a kiss from that girl.
I want magic,
The kind that falls from lips when spoken of,
And bridges minds when thought about.

Again, I don't remember when,
But I met Envy,
And she told me that everything would be fine.

People Who Try

Sometimes I let my phone die,
And relationships with it,
And I keep my motivations tinted,
Because I know that
Mistakes are made by people who try.

I've got a patience
That even makes me anxious
When life forces me to wait.

I've got an itch for freedom
America can't or won't scratch.

Deep down I know that
Art is made by people who try.

Nothing's The Same

Fear the sky,
Hate the water,
Pay the man,
Fuck the daughter,
Love the life,
Record the horrors,
And hope to remember it all.

Black at a country club,
Black in my country,
I forget myself,
My limited access to money.

Fair ain't how the world works,
Pay fare to see the world work.

Knowledge makes all the difference,
But then,
Nothing's the same

Scary Waters

She keeps her money in her bra,
Her son in her arms
And her head up.

My sister, my beautiful big sister,
Is a woman of a dead history,
Of a broken home, of pieces,
And yet she is whole.

How? I don't know,

But very rarely
Do pirates happen upon treasure,
And rarer than that
Is one who stops to ask how it was made.
So maybe the grandest lesson of life
Is such that
The unlucky people are to be coveted,
And loved like capital,
Across scary waters.

A Second Side of Things

I've accumulated a white girlfriend story.

My adoptive mother believes
This phase has put me through a wall,
And I'm stuck on what's pretty
Rather than what's beautiful.
My adoptive mother tells me she dated a Jewish boy once,
To cement her bravery and dedication
To the experiment of being Black but also living
A full life.

In my ever-growing garden of a mind,
It is a curious thing to love someone,
And more curious are green eyes and flowing brown hair.

My adoptive mom assures me that when I'm older,
I'll take darker partners.
Because a Black man ain't that without a Black woman
To love and be loved by.

I've come to the conclusion that I need help,

My girlfriend helps me celebrate confusion,
She takes a moment, spreads it across her lips,
And kisses me with it.

What she gives me isn't clarity, but it's something,

Something on the running tab of justice in my country,
That which makes the documentaries go mute,
That which favors a second side of things.

The decisions I'm pressed to make as a youth are so loud
My ears ache, and my heart hurts,
And I can either plant my feet in the here and now
Or run back to the past--
To the root of the discomfort my adoptive mother felt,
When I brought a pair of green eyes home
From school.

Eureka: A Joyous Cry

Welcome

Welcome to the broken hearts club
Where healing is not so rare that we don't sing about it,
But not so common that we know the words
To any of these songs.

Wins and Losses

The only way to control failure
Is to win,
But the only way
To control disappointment
Is to win
With the right people.

It's In You

Autonomy whispers to service,
Vivid, relenting pitches,
Under the guise of observance,
It says,

"If there's a God to be worshipped,
It's in you."

Love Is A Womb

I know that love won't always look like me,
Love is a womb--
It preaches the laws of Tetris,
Of how life has always been a matching game,
Of balance and geometry.

I know that love won't always look like me,
Love is a wound--
It preaches that whatever learns
Must hurt first.

I know that the most beautiful version of myself,
Is the ugliest, the bloodiest,
The most understanding of nature
And history.

I know that love is where everyone comes from.

New Life

I'm documenting and realizing,
I am very much alive,
But the reaper likes my skin tone.

Now, of all the times I could have died,
I don't think
I have ever been less prepared.
This new life, this good life,
It makes you want it,
That's what's scary, not the reaper.

Methuselah

Passion, oh fruit of my father, where people meet heaven,
Where trees fall from fruit and everything is okay.
Where tragedy is reversible, I sleep better after 900 years,
And I'm wise enough to not care to explain to whoever I meet
That I matter.
Where I have less to prove,
Where I tell stories and people listen, but none cry at the end.
Passion, oh fruit of my father,
Bring me the freedom he must have felt without me.

The Struggle

The struggle is such that each victory
Is small,
But also as large as our hearts,
And as hard-earned
As respect ought to be.

Can't Take A Joke

Understand that we are not subtle people,
When we shoot,
We shoot so much that we do not miss,
When we laugh it's a full-body activity.

All of our feelings except joy
Have faded to Black,
Black as thick as our skin has grown.

If you can't take a joke,
You can't take the love I have for you,
You cannot have me.

Pieces

If you collected pieces of yourself
Like you do ill thoughts and the judgment of others
I'm sure you'd find something to love.
Remember that
To seek the affection of others is to misunderstand
How feelings work,
And to beg for respect is to forget what you are begging for.
The piece of you that needs is the strongest,
Not the weakest.

What Must Have Felt Like Home

I've never felt like I was lacking in talent,
Though, I've been accused of
Overstating my understanding.

I've never felt
What must have felt like home,
Sometimes you have to
Have less
To realize there's more.

Sometimes

Forever the only Black kid somewhere,
But sometimes at peace,
Melanin enters as though she were a demon
At church.
As if to say, "I don't belong here,
But I know the bible too."
As if to force a conclusion
Or the patient hands of God,
As if to whisper work songs
And lull the suburbs to sleep.

Sometimes, when she sings,
The imagery can't help but strike me,
How the strangest fruit from the strangest trees
Sort of resembles me.

Feelings Are Instruments Too

Feelings are instruments too,
My last relationship inspired a concerto

I should really learn to dance to better music,
To love a more consistent rhythm.

White Collar

Her heart is a white-collar construction site
On which everyone is too important
To fix anything.

Her mind is a cemetery
Partially because she lives through her eyes,
But honestly, it's the lack of honesty,
And she knows it.

From This Angle

Love from this angle is mute.
She wears a red dress and she does not speak.
I remember how she felt.
She was not a soft suede or velvet to the touch,
No, more like Velcro, rugged, a binding,
A resolve to stay whole
In spite of every which way
She is torn.

America's Mandatory Pottery Class

This is America's mandatory pottery class,
The convent of being Black comes with a grief that shapes and molds
As if,
"If you would just keep your hands
Where everyone could see them,
And stay still"
Something beautiful might happen,
They might call you art
And fall away.
They might indulge your life one last time,
And mark you a fine investment,
They might decide you exist better
As a person, as an artist,
Than another news story.

Attention

I feel like my love muscles atrophied,
And my hair is too thick to run your fingers through,
And my mind is too busy to cross more than once,
You'd have to get in where you fit in,
Like the demons do.

Commitment

Peppermint promises,
Sweet, but strong on the tongue,
To commit to this energy,
Is to commit to the sun.

I hope I'm around forever to tell you,
I fuck with you,
Or less sordid,
That I'm in touch with you,
Or more dramatic,
That I'm in love with you.

So that I can hear myself breathe.

To Pimp A Caterpillar

Chevy in quicksand,
Head in my hands,
Hole in my heart,
Hole in my pants,
Dent in my car,
Keeping me humble,
Pray, I don't stumble,
Fumble, fall,
Pray through it all,

More moral than mortal man,
Who won't pardon my tan,
Been through the fire,
I know that light creates darkness
In there,

I can't really talk,
Been through it all,
They want my stories,
I want to evolve.

It's taking me higher,
Black man for hire,
Fuck a slave,
Ship, I wanna retire.
Someday.
I want to come back home.

Women

To love women,
Is to understand that
Young may be an emotion.

Is to elicit bad poetry.
Is to be inspired by everything.
Is to bite a lip that isn't yours.
Is to have another to appreciate,
What God and your mother made.

To love women,
Mistake after mistake,
Is to be ahead of whatever
Time you are passing through.

Freedom

The love between us is not lost,
It is free,
Some other where, for some other's wear
For now,
I know better than to need someone
Like you.

Bucket List

Part of my bucket list was to see it grow more,
And it did, and I'm not dead,
So I'm feeling really half-lived and lied to,
The expiration date I survived through
Feels more like my birthday than my birthday
Most years.
Life has really brought me to tears lately,
Sure, my life is crazy, but it's amazing,
Because I'm still here.
Doctor, Doctor,
Jesus, Jesus,
One of three favors, two more reasons
To make it in life,
And to accept all the help I always rejected
In spite,
Of better judgment.

Some Say

You can never cry "jump"
And find yourself over the hurdle.
Words have their power, it's true,
But the magic in them is slow-acting,
Some say we have a heart to feel,
And others say we have fingers.
Life is literal and thus we know limits,
But life is also not literal,
And thus, at times,
We find ourselves knowing even
What we do not know.

Depression Is A White People Thing

Maybe we're not there yet.
Maybe happy is still around the corner
And the groceries
Just have to come from somewhere else.
We do realize that dreams
Lose to reality more often than not,
That happy is expensive,
And people usually break if they
Can't afford it.

I was eight years old when I realized it,
And my then 16-year-old brother,
A hardened veteran,
Echoed the sentiments of the hood,

"Depression is a white people thing."

He was only half kidding,
And I guess we were lucky,
Because we knew better

Back Scratcher Blues

I've got the back scratcher blues,
I'm all supply and no demand to some of you,
Friendships be one sided,
Thoughts collidin' but star-studded,
Like Calliope,
Under it, I kind of made my own Island,
I'll say hi, but then it's bye again,

I don't think I can trust you to need me,
And I don't want to be greedy,
I'll always let you go.

On Love

Love is the damp corner of a dark room
Where the bugs come in.
It is potential on ice in a rink
That no one seems to have brought
The right shoes for.
I mean it is inconvenient, funny,
Poorly timed, full of uneven steps,
And unwanted company.

I'm still seventeen, so chew my words
Before you swallow them,
But understand me when I say,
However clumsily and in juvenile tender,
That I care, and it's nice, and it hurts,
And I call it love.

Cut Different

Dry eyes belong to people with lesser ambitions,
You were cut different,
Find the rest of your fold.

Exactly As I Am

My friend is an artist,
And upon her request to draw me,
I requested that she color me
Angry, resolute, and painfully aware.
Color me brown, or black,
Experienced,
Exactly as I am.

Eulogy: A Death

Purity

I've seen offense in its purest form:
A tiny piece of metal that expands
To form a funeral around a future
That is now only used as a campsite
For regret.

Teddy bears and balloons
Won't ever mean what they used to.

So when I say be safe,
What I really mean is,
Don't make me have to
Buy your mother flowers
And sing about you.

Appreciate You Still

I appreciate you still,
The way a rabbit would a dog.
I had no idea I could run this fast.

On my way,
I found a piece of you untapped,
I found a man in me
That had your freckles, your eyes, your nose,
But not your face,
Not the weight of bastard life,
Or the sinful nature
Of the circumstances that inspired me.

I found myself.
A path to another path
Inside me.
I found everything good.
I found everything worth your absence.

Who Knew

I feel like I'm falling from
A high place,
I used to think of
As low to the ground.

I feel like the right thing
Is too far from easy
To be done or considered,

I'm hurt, but harder now.

Who knew patience
Was an action word?
Who knew anything
But hurt?

American Pie

Upon hearing the phrase
"Life is like a slice of pie,"
I'd rediscovered the importance
Of playing with my food.

I'd like whoever is in charge
To explain to me
Why some slices are sweeter than others,
And why my little cousin
Ate his so fast.

The Needs Of A Child

I'm sure the needs of a child
Are complex things,

But let this be said about angry people,
Who were once angry children,

In my experience, which is hardened,
And vast, and trauma-filled,
And capped at 17 revolutions
Around the sun.

Angry children, as I know them,
As I am them,
Are almost always angry
At how quickly
"I'm sorry," becomes
"I'm doing the best I can."

Memory

Color blindness is still blindness,
Not immune to the way the world works.

You are but a sour memory
You cannot devolve from,
Or come out of,

And you would rather
Take my memory, my identity,
The context of my being,
And reduce it--

You would close your eyes,
Close your mind to history,
And tell me
"It doesn't matter that you're Black"

And I laugh,
Because I understand how much
We have in common.
Everyone I know
Would rather erase their mistakes too.

It is why I write in pencil,
But our forefathers wrote in pen

When they built this country--

They wrote what they wanted to last forever,
And in one of those immortal lines,
Was my own sour memory,
The exploitation of my people.

Where you have guilt,
I have nothing.
I have missing time,
Missing family,
Gaps in education,
No financial literacy,
A hyphen for a national name,

And you judge me for struggling,
For forgetting
What you did not want me to remember
In the first place--

That I am a Negro, a Black,
An African-American
Which means--
No, which has always meant--
That I can either
Lay down and die,
Or work harder than anyone
Should ever have to--

Just to be treated with favor.

BayBra

BayBra

Translation: Baby Brother

Translation: Little Mistake

Translation: Mom came home drunk again 17 year ago

Translation: I love you anyway

After The Party

We smoke up and talk down, right?
Why mean what we say, when we could clown?
The girls here just want to laugh anyway,
And God is always late.

It shows up after the party,
Ready to save the souls we gave away
A while ago
To keep the drinks cold,
The blunts rolled,
And the bodies warm.
Behavior that's proof of cycles it created
Even it couldn't escape from.
Proof that proofs like proof of income
Matters more than it should at the bottom,

I'm sure that whenever God reaches us,
It, too, will be tired.

Glitter

Heartbreaker, heartbreaker, please,
Where's the love and the peace?
Put more potential in my middle finger,
Give me reasons to leave.

I saw the blood on the sheets,
I've seen the girls on your Instagram,
I know who you want to be.
I can see how you see,

Yourself in tight jeans and tighter spirits,
You're still the brightest spirit I know,
Irreconcilable good, with reconcilable goals,
Enough to bury your woes,
Head to toe in glitter.

Here Today Gone Today

Mortality checked, reality hit
And took our brothers with it.
Now we laugh a little different.

Some of us are here today
And gone today,
So every tomorrow, we celebrate,
In old fashioned lung clasping,
Liver burning
And pole dancing action.

Black Blood runs different in grief.

Trauma

Trauma is not the moments of, but the moments after.
It is not the act, it is what comes after the act.
It is not my father leaving, it's my father being gone.
It is not the bullet, it's the death.
It's the crazy,
Because how the fuck does anyone say anything these days,
Except, "I'm sorry" or "try to forget about it."

I'm Not Trying So Hard Anymore

People will use you
Until you're gone.
The most basic instinct we possess
Is to possess.
I thought I'd always want to make you feel good,
I think you thought that too--
I think what made you red,
Is what also made me blue.
It's like I blew,
And I'm not trying so hard anymore.

Behind the Garage

I owe you a red nose and some face paint,
I owe you love, from the corner store,
Jamaican beef patties and honey buns.
I owe you a few more years of thought,
Some shoe laces, and canned okra.
I owe you a life lived well, and full,
And that kiss behind the garage,
I owe you rejection, and confidence,
And sex.
I owe you an era in humanity
Where life is sacred.

And when I leave this earth
To find you,
I'll pay you back in full,
For what your death taught me.

Ambition

My little cousins think
Ambition comes from the waist down.
I think it comes from where we come from,
But they never listen when I say that.
I think we're all connected,
But some connections are stronger than others.
I know what the bottom feels like.
The taste of pavement is always as fresh
As the tongue you sport.
Some black boys with purple lips
Learn the speech patterns of night time,
To coax their livelihoods to sleep,
While they stay up,
To protect themselves,
And never dare to dream.
I think ambition is the courage
To take a nap when you have doubts
About waking up.
It's that football filled with faith
That we learn to throw far into the future.
It's that girl we settle down with.
It's that project we're working on.
It's that conversation in the barbershop
About who's going to win the play-offs.
All of these things wear the shadow
Of the promise to ourselves,
That we are going to make it.

No One Lied To Me

I left my pride on the doorstep of a friend's home,
I misplaced it early,
Like I would have had I been born
Anyone else.

I used to tell myself bedtime stories
To convince myself
That I'd wake up the next day,
Or to downplay its importance,
Almost out of consideration
For my dead friends.

In that I learned the conundrum of memories,
Why everyone wants to be here,
And not the past or even the future,
Because people forget things.

Though, on my worst days, I remember,
How no one lied to me growing up,
No one told me
That everything was going to be fine.

Graduation

Fat kid, Black kid, double whammy,
I come from family that can't vote,
My genetics is felony.
Heaven been failin' me lately.

I watched my uncle die, crazy.

He was foaming at the mouth,
I held onto the couch as he fell to the ground,
Now he's a memory.

I lost my virginity that weekend, and my cousin.
We was buggin', shit was fun,
And I was nothin' but a kid
Who couldn't love right,
So I took that first light and snuffed it.

My friends were murderers,
Killing time, brain cells, and records,
Wannabe rappers,
Our lives wouldn't let us.

That weekend was magic,
Everything had happened so fast,
I couldn't live it all sober.

Heaven got closer,
As we poured our youth into Styrofoam cups,
And told our parents it was juice.

We never felt it was enough,
So we would go outside and shoot,
Hoops,
Or people in later years.
I made it out--but I can't speak on what David did.
I'm still in the drought,
But, I've got money and love,
And no fucks for all the hate I'd give.

I never know what to say when people ask me
How I made it here.
I'm not okay, I'm hardly facing fear.
Success is kind of tight on me,
But the low hangin' fruit never did right for me.
And I got pride now,
A result of dignity,
And depression testin' my faith, and ability.

This is recess after graduation.
I'm a foster care alumni--I can swing when I want to,
Hit the park and feel the breeze whenever I feel like.

The things I could tell you,
I could make your head spin.

And I feel powerful now,
'Cuz I was powerless then.

I wrap my actions in plastic so I know you hear it,
Swear, the success on this kid
Is just enough to fear him,
The rebellion is so obvious,
Baggy clothes cuz I don't mean to look pretty,
Heavy soul because I had to do so much
On my own.

And I would call myself successful,
But more than that,
I would call myself tired.

I Could Have Really Used A Father

Waste a seed and grow a tree I guess,

A baby boy that looks like me I guess,

If I'm honest, I could have really used a father,

Mama could have really used a partner,

My brother always needed a man his own size

To spar with.

It felt like Sparta without you,

I saw as mama grew tired,

I had no morals or values,

I must be hell bound too,

For all the shit I did,

I'm nicer now,

When I needed you I was a different kid.

About The Metal

I knew a kid who was a ghost before 18,
But by your logic,
My being young precludes me
From the tragedy of ending.

I am young, it's true
But the threat of death,
Has a unique way of aging a person.
It's a dark night every time I think about it.

How stray metal doesn't discriminate,
Unlike employers.
You can ask my mother 'bout the employers,
And I wish you could ask my cousin,
About the metal.

Pretend Deep

When life gives you lemons,
Ask for your cousin back.
Say you'll make whatever, lemonade,
Or even a hundred racks
For him to feel okay again.

Pretend deep.

Go to church on Sundays,
Tell the worshipers that life told you,
"One day,
The fruit I bring will be sweeter."
As forget to mean it.

'Cuz it could come back with zucchini
And you would have to eat it.

I Rhyme To Make It Easier

When lips move, bodies drop.
Celebrating life with vodka,
'Cuz the homie got body shots.
The city let his body rot for 2 hours
Before they came.

Ain't nobody seen it but they heard it,
All that screamin' down the way.

I've seen some things I can't forget,
That shit be eatin' at my brain.
I express myself like this,
But people got so much to say.

I rhyme to make it easier,
Because things are not okay.
It feels like
I'm the only one who has the strength
To say that.

Good People Be Damned

So much evil counts on the fact
That you might not make enough
A year
At your 9 to 5 to be a hero.

When you're broke,
Compassion typically ranges from
One to zero.

All the love at the bottom
Floats to the top,
Just like the cash and eventually,
The backdrop of every coke rock too,

Good people be damned,
And sent to heaven too soon.

The Term The Psychiatrists Use

Physical abuse, the term the psychiatrists use
We called it gettin' our asses beat,
Mama called it rhythm and blues.

I'm hyper-physical
Because otherwise I'd have never learned
To be gentle,
 And no one wants that other part of me,
So I made it hard to see.

When I was younger I read this article,
About arteries,
and how everything in the body
Works together for the health of the whole.
And still, there are days when I'd rather
Do to my liver and my lungs
What's been done to me.

I guess I'm not much help to the whole,
But I'm learning.

Write 'em Away

How far is gone?
I have family down there, and a few friends,
I'd love to visit,
But then again, I really like my room.
I have this problem with commitment,
And it keeps me away from high places,
But most days,
I can't see how the ground is any better.

I love you,
Is a game that I play with myself,
It's why I could tell that you were lying,
I heard your voice like I hear mine, and you turned red.
I fell from stairs that I don't remember climbing,
And my problem had vanished,
It was that easy, for the both of us,

Honesty isn't a burden,
It's a chance to let go,
The weight was added when
We decided not to.

Bird Cage

Grievances us sons inherit
Like freckles,
Commitment issues,
And an affinity to violence,
Are many and particularly heavy crosses to carry
Uphill,
Into academia, success, pussy,
Or wherever you're headed next.

I get it though—
Too hard around the edges
And too soft at the core,
Is the way lesser men fold
And the cookie crumbles
As though my father was a baker
And my mother was an oven—
She would overheat often,
And never made much noise,
Not until you pressed her.

If I were a woman, I would not be her type.
If I were a man,
I would rip my heart out and cut my dick off,
And tell God I'm sorry,
I just wanted a better shot
At being a good person,
A fairer shot at not becoming my father.
But you can only run so far
From a single point on a dotted line
Before you end up next to it again.

So to be clear:
I do like my freckles.
I do love my mother.
I do not know my father well enough
To call what I feel for him love,
But if I were searching for a compromise
For the sake of this poem,
I could find it.

I could say he was a fire-breathing dragon
Who burned everything
But having been born part dragon gave me wings.
I could say he taught me everything about being there,
By not being there.
I could thank him
For the tragic ascension from black boy to story—
Success or otherwise.

I am a metaphorical campfire guitarist,
A podium and microphone enthusiast,
I am loud, the center of attention,
A pterodactyl under a fake sky,

I am airplane noise.

I am a bird in a cage—
And now that I know it,
This cage will not hold me for much longer.

Stories

My depression is the dark
After a short day,
A colorless void,
That always has time and room,
For me.
It told me bedtime stories
When I was too young to understand
Why my father was never there
To tell me bedtime stories,
Stories that kept me awake,
Stories that kept me alive,
Stories that kept me,
Stories that I learned,
Survived through, and tell everyday
I find myself missing the dark.

Once You Get It They Move It

Glorified ashtrays and cup holders we are,
Of things that absorb,
And do not burn.

To break down and break down again,
Swisher guts in a solo cup,
My heart,
Behind some white picket fence
I had just recently learned to want.

There's not enough dream-space
For all the dreams that I keep folding,
There's not enough air in my lungs
To filter out
All the heat that I've been holding.

Once you get it,
That elusive and hard-come-by thing,
Through trials of justice, fire,
And other error,
They move it,
So you are never keeping up
Enough.

Made in the USA
Monee, IL
18 July 2020